Farm Facts

Animals on the Farm

by Lisa J. Amstutz

raintree
a Capstone company — publishers for children

Raintree is an imprint of Capstone Global Library Limited, a company incorporated in England and Wales having its registered office at 264 Banbury Road, Oxford, OX2 7DY – Registered company number: 6695582

www.raintree.co.uk
myorders@raintree.co.uk

Edited by Jill Kalz
Picture research by Kelly Garvin
Originated by Capstone Global Library

Designed by Ashlee Suker
Production by Katy LaVigne
Printed and bound in India

ISBN 978 1 4747 6866 5 (hardback)   ISBN 978 1 4747 6882 5 (paperback)

British Library Cataloguing in Publication Data
A full catalogue record for this book is available from the British Library.

Acknowledgements
We would like to thank the following for permission to reproduce photographs: iStockphoto/pixdeluxe, 5; Shutterstock: Anastasija Popova, 13, bagicat, 1 (right), Baronb, cover, BIGANDT.COM, 19, jadimages, 1 (left), Julia Lototskaya, 10, kevin leah, 15, Leo D, 8, monticello, 14, photoshooter2015, 21, r.classen, backcover, 6, sixpixx, 16, smereka, 7, 9, talseN, 11, William John Hunter, 17, yevgeniy11, 20
Design Element: Shutterstock: Dudarev Mikhail, J.Schelkle, K.Narloch-Liberra, laura.h, Sichon

Every effort has been made to contact copyright holders of material reproduced in this book. Any omissions will be rectified in subsequent printings if notice is given to the publisher.

Contents

Living together

Farmers and their families live on farms. Who else lives there? Lots of farm animals!

Making milk

Cows graze on grass. They also eat grain and hay. Cows make milk. The farmer milks them every day.

Goats make milk too.
Their milk can be
made into cheese
and yogurt.

Sharing the farm

Pigs have snouts and curly tails.
They use their snouts to look for
tasty things to eat.
Pigs roll in mud
to keep cool.

Horses have long, strong legs. They can run fast. In the old days, horses would pull farm machinery. Now people ride them for fun.

Chickens lay eggs.
Farmers collect the eggs.
Eggs can be white,
brown or
even blue!

We get wool from sheep. Wool is warm and soft. Farmers shear the sheep to collect the wool.

Sheepdogs are trained to round up the sheep. They move the flock of sheep from one field to another field.

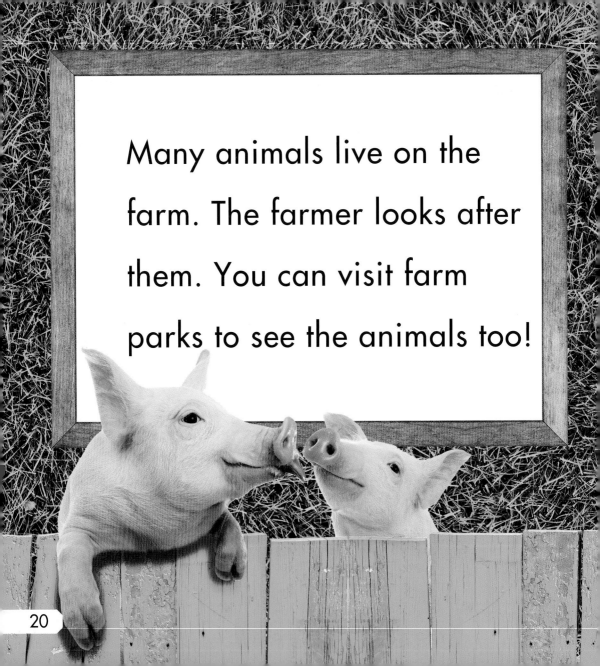

Many animals live on the farm. The farmer looks after them. You can visit farm parks to see the animals too!

Glossary

grain   the seed of a grassy plant, such as wheat, rice, corn, rye or barley

flock   group of sheep

graze   to feed on grass

hay   dried grass

shear   cut off the wool from a sheep

snout   the long, front part of an animal's head, including the nose, mouth and jaws

wool   the soft, thick hair of sheep or goats; wool is used to make yarn

Find out more

Books

A Nature Walk on the Farm (Nature Walks), Louise and Richard Spilsbury (Raintree, 2015)

Cows and Their Calves (Animal Offspring) Margaret Hall (Raintree, 2018)

Farm Animals, Joanne Mattern (National Geographic Kids, 2017)

Websites

Discover lots of farm animal facts and fun craft activities:
www.activityvillage.co.uk/farm-animals

Watch a video of a working farm:
www.bbc.com/bitesize/clips/z9qtfg8

Comprehension questions

1. What are two farm animals in this book that make milk?

2. Why do pigs roll in mud?

3. How do some dogs help farmers?

Index

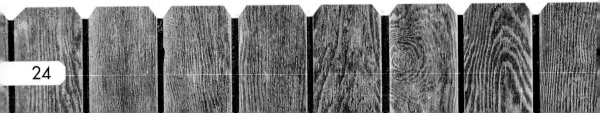